The Book of Intriguing Facts for Smart Kids

Science, Geography and Earth Wonders

Morgan Adams

Contents

Introduction

Hello there, smarty-pants! Yes, I'm talking to YOU.

Welcome to a book that's about to make your brain go, "Whoa!"

This isn't your average boring textbook full of blah-blah science and yawn-worthy geography.

Nope, this is a treasure trove of amazing, hilarious, and sometimes downright weird facts about the world, the universe, and everything in between.

You're about to discover the kind of things that will make you the smartest person in the room. Like, did you know there's a jellyfish that can live forever? Or that there's a town in Norway where it's illegal to die? (Seriously. Look it up.)

Being curious is a superpower. Even Albert Einstein, one of the smartest people ever, once said, *"I have no special talents. I am only passionately curious."* So, if you're curious, congrats—you're already halfway to genius level!

This book isn't just about cramming your brain with facts. It's about showing you how incredible, strange, and flat-out amazing the world is. We're talking about:

★ Science facts that will make you say, "Wait, WHAT?"

★ Geography that'll take you to the ends of the Earth (and beyond).

★ Earth wonders that prove nature has a seriously creative imagination.

Oh, and it's not just for you. Your parents, teachers, and even your dog (if they can read) will be impressed when you casually drop facts like, "Did you know bananas are berries, but strawberries aren't?" Minds = blown.

Stephen Hawking, another super-genius, once said, *"Look up at the stars, not down at your feet."* Translation: Always stay curious, keep exploring, and don't step in gum.

There are no rules. Flip to any page, dive into any fact, and get ready to have your mind blown. You don't have to read it in order (who even does that?). It's like a buffet of awesome—you can pick and choose the parts that interest you the most.

Each chapter is packed with bite-sized nuggets of knowledge that are perfect for:

★ Impressing your friends at lunch.

★ Annoying your parents with "Did you know?" questions.

★ Starting your journey to becoming the next Einstein or Marie Curie.

Before we start, let's test your brainpower with a riddle:

I'm not alive, but I grow. I don't have lungs, but I need air. What am I?

(Hint: You'll find the answer somewhere in this book. See? Curiosity already activated!)

So, what are you waiting for? Grab a snack, find a cozy spot, and get ready to explore the most incredible things this planet—and the universe—has to offer.

Chapter 1

Mind-Bending Science Facts

Weird States of Matter (Beyond Solid, Liquid, and Gas)

You've probably heard about the three main states of matter: solid, liquid, and gas. But what if I told you there are *more* states of matter? Yep, science isn't just playing tricks on you—there are some seriously weird states of matter that don't fit into the usual categories. Let's explore!

The Classics: Solid, Liquid, and Gas

Quick refresher:

- ★ **Solids**: They're sturdy. They keep their shape. Like your phone or that cookie you're about to eat (if you haven't already).

- ★ **Liquids**: They flow. They take the shape of their container. Like water, juice, or melted ice cream on a hot day.

- ★ **Gases**: They're free spirits. They zoom around and don't stick to one shape, like the air you breathe or helium in a balloon.

Got it? Great. Now, get ready to have your mind blown, because these are just the beginning.

Plasma: The Fourth State (Not the TV Kind)

What it is: Plasma is like gas's wild cousin—it's supercharged. Imagine taking a gas and zapping it with so much energy that the atoms break apart, creating a soup of particles called ions. Sounds intense, right?

Where you'll find it:

- ★ The Sun is made of plasma (which explains why it's so hot).

- ★ Neon signs glow because of plasma inside them.

- ★ Lightning? That's plasma too!

Fun Fact: Plasma makes up 99% of the visible universe. So, technically, you're surrounded by plasma, even though you can't see most of it.

Bose-Einstein Condensate (BEC): Matter's Chillest Form

What it is: BEC happens when you take a bunch of atoms and cool them down to *just a tiny bit above absolute zero* (the coldest temperature possible). When they get this cold, the atoms stop acting like individuals and start behaving as one giant "super-atom."

Where you'll find it: Mostly in science labs, because it's tricky to create. Scientists first made BEC in 1995, so it's like the baby of the matter family.

Fun Fact: Albert Einstein and an Indian scientist named Satyendra Nath Bose predicted BEC's existence way back in the 1920s. They didn't get to see it themselves, but their genius made it possible.

Superfluid: The Liquid That Defies Gravity

What it is: A superfluid is a liquid that flows without any resistance. Imagine pouring water that never slows down, even on a flat surface. It can even climb up walls and drip out of containers *upside down*. What?!

Where you'll find it: Superfluid helium, a kind of liquid helium, is often used in super-cool experiments (literally).

Fun Fact: Superfluids are so weird that they can spin forever without stopping. They're like the Energizer Bunny of liquids!

Quark-Gluon Plasma: The Beginning of Everything

What it is: This is what the universe was made of right after the Big Bang—an incredibly hot, super-dense soup of tiny particles called quarks and gluons. It's like the "baby food" of the universe!

Where you'll find it: In particle accelerators like the Large Hadron Collider, where scientists recreate the conditions of the early universe.

Fun Fact: Quark-gluon plasma is hotter than the Sun—trillions of degrees hot! It's like nature's ultimate hot sauce.

Time Crystals: The Newest Kid on the Block

What it is: Time crystals sound like something from a sci-fi movie, but they're real. They're structures that repeat in time instead of space. Basically, they "tick" like a clock without using any energy.

Where you'll find it: In fancy quantum labs for now. Scientists only discovered them in 2016, so they're still figuring out what they can do.

Fun Fact: Time crystals might one day help make quantum computers even more powerful. So, yes, the future is officially here.

How Do These States of Matter Work?

Great question! It all comes down to *energy*. The more energy you add (or take away) from atoms, the weirder they behave. That's why we get solids, liquids, gases, and all these super-cool extras.

Test Your Knowledge!

Here's a challenge for you:

1. What state of matter is the Sun made of?
2. What's the weirdest thing a superfluid can do?
3. What temperature do scientists need to create Bose-Einstein Condensate?

You can find the answers as you keep exploring this book. Or just impress your family by explaining why lightning is plasma at dinner tonight.

What it is: Is it a liquid? Is it a solid? It's both! Liquid crystals flow like liquids but have the organized structure of solids. Imagine a marching parade, but instead of people, it's molecules that can flow and wiggle.

Where you'll find it: In your TV, phone, or tablet screen! Yep, the "LCD" in your LCD screen stands for **Liquid Crystal Display.** Without these supercool substances, we wouldn't have the fancy screens we use every day.

Fun Fact: Liquid crystals are super sensitive to temperature changes, which is why they're also used in mood rings. So, your "blue means calm" mood ring is actually powered by science!

Fermionic Condensates: BEC's Even Cooler Cousin

What it is: Remember Bose-Einstein Condensates (BEC)? Well, Fermionic condensates are just as cold and bizarre, but they're made from particles called fermions instead of bosons. (Don't worry, you don't need to know the difference to appreciate the coolness!)

These condensates act in ways that defy the rules of physics—like sliding through each other without ever touching. Mind = blown.

Where you'll find it: In cutting-edge physics labs. It's so rare that even most scientists haven't worked with it.

Fun Fact: Fermionic condensates could help unlock the secrets of superconductors, which might one day lead to trains that levitate and zoom around like something from a sci-fi movie.

Strange Matter: From the Hearts of Stars

What it is: Deep inside neutron stars—those super-dense remnants of exploded stars—there might be something called "strange matter." It's made up of particles called strange quarks (yes, that's their actual name), and it's one of the densest forms of matter in the universe.

Where you'll find it: Only in the hearts of neutron stars. You're not likely to bump into it at your local science museum.

Fun Fact: Strange matter is so dense that a sugar-cube-sized chunk of it would weigh more than Mount Everest. Imagine trying to carry THAT in your lunchbox!

Superconductors: The Zero-Resistance Superstars

What it is: Superconductors are materials that can conduct electricity without losing any energy. Normally, electricity leaks a little bit when it moves through wires, but superconductors say, "Nope, not on my watch!"

Where you'll find it: In MRI machines, particle accelerators, and maybe one day in super-fast transportation systems.

Fun Fact: Superconductors work best at super cold temperatures, close to absolute zero. But scientists are working hard to create ones that work at room temperature.

Glass: The Solid That's Not Quite Solid

What it is: You might think glass is a solid, but technically, it's something called an *amorphous solid*. Unlike true solids, which have neatly arranged molecules, glass has molecules that are all jumbled up—kind of like a frozen liquid.

Where you'll find it: Look around! Windows, mirrors, and your favorite drinking glass are all examples.

Fun Fact: Really old glass, like the kind in ancient windows, sometimes looks thicker at the bottom because it's slowly flowing downward over centuries.

Dark Matter: The Invisible Mystery

What it is: Dark matter isn't a state of matter you can touch or see, but it's out there. Scientists believe it makes up about 27% of the universe, but they still don't know exactly what it is. It doesn't emit light, which makes it *invisible*. Spooky, right?

Where you'll find it: Everywhere! Even in the space between stars and galaxies.

Fun Fact: Dark matter doesn't interact with normal matter (like you or me), which is why we don't notice it. It's kind of like a ghost haunting the universe.

Metallic Hydrogen: A Superpowered Solid

What it is: Normally, hydrogen is a gas. But under insane pressure—like inside giant planets such as Jupiter—it turns into a solid metal. Metallic hydrogen is super shiny, conducts electricity, and might one day be used to make rocket fuel.

Where you'll find it: Deep in the cores of Jupiter and Saturn. Scientists are still trying to create it on Earth.

Fun Fact: Metallic hydrogen could help us make super-efficient batteries and engines. Imagine powering a car that could go to the Moon and back on a single charge!

Why Does Matter Get So Weird?

All these funky states of matter are the result of extreme conditions—like super high pressure, incredibly low temperatures, or gigantic magnetic fields. When atoms and particles are pushed to their limits, they start to behave in ways that don't make sense to us. And that's what makes science so amazing!

A Quick Recap

Here's what we've learned so far about the weird and wonderful states of matter:

1. Plasma is a supercharged gas (hello, lightning!).

2. Bose-Einstein Condensates and Fermionic Condensates are ultra-cold and super weird.

3. Superfluids climb walls like Spider-Man.

4. Strange matter is incredibly dense and found in neutron stars.

5. Dark matter is invisible but makes up most of the universe.

Your Turn to Wonder

Imagine you've just discovered a brand-new state of matter. What would you name it? What cool things could it do? Would it help power spaceships? Glow in the dark? Or maybe make the perfect pizza?

Gravity: The Basics

Gravity is a force that pulls objects toward each other. The bigger the object, the stronger its pull. That's why tiny things like paperclips don't stick to you, but gigantic planets can keep you firmly on the ground.

Isaac Newton (a super-smart scientist from the 1600s) figured this out when an apple allegedly fell on his head. True story? Maybe not, but it's a fun way to remember he discovered gravity. He even said, *"What goes up must come down,"* which is basically gravity in a nutshell.

Why Don't We Float Away?

Earth is like a giant magnet, and gravity is its pull. Every time you jump, gravity yanks you back down. Without gravity, we'd all float off into space like balloons. (Sounds fun, but trust me—you'd miss being able to sit down without drifting away.)

Fun Fact: If you went to the Moon, you'd weigh about 1/6 of what you weigh on Earth because the Moon's gravity is much weaker. That means you could jump six times higher there. Space basketball, anyone?

Gravity Around the Solar System

Gravity isn't the same everywhere. Each planet has its own level of gravity, depending on its size and mass. Let's take a quick trip around the solar system and see how gravity measures up:

- ★ **Mercury:** Gravity here is weaker than Earth's, so you'd feel lighter—but not as light as on the Moon.

- ★ **Jupiter:** Whoa! Gravity on Jupiter is *so strong* that you'd weigh over twice as much as you do on Earth. Good luck trying to jump there!

- ★ **Mars:** Mars has less gravity than Earth, so you'd feel lighter and could jump much farther. Space explorers will probably have a lot of fun playing games on Mars someday.

Fun Fact: Astronauts on the International Space Station seem to float because they're in constant freefall around Earth, but gravity is still pulling them down. It's like they're on a roller coaster that never ends!

Gravity in Space: Black Holes

We can't talk about gravity without mentioning black holes. These are areas in space where gravity is so strong that *nothing* can escape—not even light. Imagine if someone turned gravity up to a million and then added more. Boom, black hole.

Black holes form when massive stars collapse under their own weight. They might sound scary, but don't worry—they're really far away from Earth. In fact, the nearest black hole is about 1,000 light-years away.

Fun Fact: Scientists took the first photo of a black hole in 2019. It looks like a glowing donut, but instead of sprinkles, it's made of gas and light being sucked in by gravity.

Microgravity: Life in Freefall

Ever heard of microgravity? That's what astronauts experience when they're in space. It's not that gravity disappears—it's just much weaker. This makes everything float around, which sounds awesome until you try to eat a sandwich and your bread floats away.

Fun Fact: Astronauts practice living in microgravity by training underwater. Water's buoyancy gives them a taste of what floating in space feels like.

Weird Gravity Tricks

Gravity isn't just about keeping your feet on the ground. It also does some seriously strange things:

1.   **Tides:** Gravity from the Moon pulls on Earth's oceans, creating high and low tides. Without the Moon, the beach would be a lot less exciting!

2.   **Time Slows Down:** Gravity can actually slow down time. If you lived near a black hole, time would move more slowly for you than for someone farther away. It's called time dilation, and it's super trippy.

3.   **Mountains Affect Gravity:** Did you know gravity is slightly stronger near massive mountains? So, if you climbed Mount Everest, you'd experience a tiny bit more gravity at the top.

What If Gravity Disappeared?

Let's imagine a world without gravity for a second. It would be chaos!

★ Your cereal would float out of the bowl and into the air.

★ Cars, people, and buildings would drift into the sky.

★ Even Earth's atmosphere would float away, which means no air to breathe. Yikes!

Gravity might seem like a boring, everyday thing, but without it, life as we know it wouldn't exist.

Test Your Gravity Knowledge!

1.   Why is gravity on Jupiter stronger than on Earth?

2.   What happens to time near a black hole?

3.   Where would you feel lighter—on Mars or on the Moon?

Keep these questions in your orbit, and see if you can stump your friends with your newfound gravity expertise!

Where Science Gets Seriously Wild!

These are the kinds of facts that will make your teachers say "How did you know that?" and your friends say "No way!"

Your Body is Actually an Alien Colony! ☻

Hold onto your socks, because this is going to blow your mind: There are more bacteria living in and on your body than there are people on Earth! That's right – you're basically walking around with a whole planet of tiny organisms!

Fun Fact: The bacteria in your gut weigh about as much as a large carrot!

Try This Safe Experiment: Make a model of your gut bacteria:

1.   Get a clear jar

2.   Fill it with water

3.   Add different colored sprinkles

4.   Each sprinkle represents one type of bacteria

(Don't eat the sprinkles after – this is for science!)

Space is Full of Smelly Surprises! ✴
Guess what? Space smells like raspberries and burnt toast! Astronauts who've been on spacewalks say different parts of space have different smells. The center of our galaxy apparently smells like rum! (But please don't try to lick any meteors to check!)

Mind-Bending Space Facts:

★ One day on Venus is longer than its year!

- ★ Jupiter has at least 79 moons (Earth is jealous!)
- ★ Saturn could float in a bathtub (if you had a bathtub big enough!)

Your Brain is the World's Best Computer

Your brain is so amazing that:

- ★ It can generate enough electricity to power a small light bulb
- ★ It processes information faster than the world's fastest computer
- ★ It can store about 2.5 million gigabytes of information!

Try This Brain Game: Close your eyes and try to:

1. Remember what you had for breakfast
2. Picture your best friend's face
3. Imagine your favorite smell Congratulations! You just accessed your brain's amazing storage system!

Animal Facts That Will Make You Go "WHAT?!"

Giraffe Tongues:

- ★ They're blue-black in color
- ★ They're about 50 cm long
- ★ They're antimicrobial (that means self-cleaning!)

Penguin Superpowers:

- ★ They can shoot poop up to 4 feet away! (Gross but true!)
- ★ They propose with pebbles
- ★ Some of them are taller than you!

Chemistry Magic in Your Kitchen!

Did You Know:

- ★ Salt raises water's boiling point
- ★ Honey never spoils (they found edible honey in ancient Egyptian tombs!)
- ★ Banana peels can polish silver (but let's leave that job to grown-ups)

The World's Weirdest Materials 🔬

Aerogel:

- ★ It's 99.8% air
- ★ It can hold up a brick while weighing almost nothing
- ★ Scientists call it "frozen smoke"

Hydrophobic Sand:

- ★ It's sand that's afraid of water!
- ★ Water bounces right off it
- ★ It stays completely dry underwater

Make Your Own Non-Newtonian Fluid!

Safe experiment with adult supervision: Mix cornstarch and water to make a liquid that:

★ Acts like a liquid when you touch it slowly

★ Turns solid when you hit it

★ Goes back to liquid when you stop!

Plant Power! 🌱

★ Some plants can count!

★ A single tree can produce enough oxygen for 4 people

The Speed Champions 🏃♂

★ Cheetah: Fastest land animal (70 mph)

★ Peregrine Falcon: Fastest bird (240 mph when diving!)

★ Light: Fastest thing ever (186,282 miles per SECOND!)

Try This Speed Comparison

1. Run as fast as you can for 5 seconds

2. Count how many steps you took

3. In that same time, light could have gone around Earth 37 times!

Weird Water Facts 💧

- ★ Hot water freezes faster than cold water sometimes (it's called the Mpemba effect)
- ★ Water can exist as solid, liquid, and gas all at the same time (it's called the triple point)
- ★ There's the same amount of water on Earth now as when dinosaurs roamed!

Science Mystery Corner 🔍

Things Scientists Still Don't Know:

- ★ Why we yawn (and why it's contagious!)
- ★ Where eels come from (seriously, it's still a mystery!)
- ★ Why cats purr (they do it when happy AND when hurt!)

Your Turn to Be a Scientist!

Keep a "Weird Science Journal" where you:

1. Write down questions about things you observe
2. Research possible answers
3. Design safe experiments to test your ideas
4. Share your discoveries!

Quick Quiz!

1. Which animal has a blue-black tongue?
2. What ancient food never spoils?

3.   How fast is light?

Fire: The Living Flame

Fire might not be alive, but it sure acts like it! It grows when it's fed fuel and oxygen, and it "dies" when it runs out of energy. Fire needs three things to keep going: heat, fuel (like wood or gas), and oxygen. Without one of these, poof—no fire.

Fun Fact: Flames come in different colors depending on how hot they are. Blue flames are the hottest, while red or orange flames are cooler. (But don't touch—cooler flames are still really hot!)

Think About It: Fire can grow and spread, but it doesn't breathe or eat like living things. Isn't that wild?

Crystals: Nature's Growing Art

Crystals are stunning natural wonders that can grow into incredible shapes—but they're not alive either. Crystals form when minerals in water start to stick together. Over time, they grow into solid shapes, like the colorful gems you see in geodes.

Fun Fact: The largest crystal cave ever discovered is in Mexico. Some of its crystals are as big as buses!

Think About It: Crystals grow slowly over time, like a sculpture made by nature itself. No lungs, no brain—just pure science magic.

Mold: The Creepy Crawler That Grows Everywhere

Have you ever left a piece of bread out too long and noticed green fuzz growing on it? That's mold—a type of fungus. Mold spreads by releasing tiny spores into the air, which then land on food and start growing.

Fun Fact: Some types of mold are actually useful! Penicillin, the first antibiotic, was discovered from a mold.

Think About It: Mold might not look alive, but it thrives when it has the right conditions—just like fire or crystals.

Coral: The Colorful Builders of the Ocean

Did you know that coral is alive? Well, sort of. The coral structures you see in the ocean are actually made up of tiny living animals called polyps. These polyps build hard, stone-like skeletons around themselves to stay safe.

Fun Fact: Coral reefs grow so slowly that it can take hundreds of years to form a single reef.

Rust: The Slow-Motion Grower

When metal gets wet and exposed to air, it starts to rust. Rust spreads across the surface of the metal, making it look reddish and flaky. It's like the metal is growing a crusty coat, even though it's not alive.

Fun Fact: The Statue of Liberty is green because of a type of rust called patina. The copper on her surface reacted with the air and water to create the green color we see today.

Think About It: Rust spreads when oxygen and moisture combine—a slow, creeping transformation.

Bubbles: Temporary Magic

Bubbles are delicate spheres made of water and soap, and they only stick around for a short time before they pop. While they last, bubbles grow as you blow air into them and float through the air like tiny globes.

Fun Fact: If you add a little glycerin to your bubble mixture, your bubbles will last longer. Try it out during your next bubble-blowing adventure!

Icebergs: Frozen Giants

Icebergs are giant chunks of ice that break off glaciers and float in the ocean. They're constantly changing shape as they melt or collide with other icebergs.

Fun Fact: Only about 10% of an iceberg is visible above the water. The rest is hidden beneath the surface!

Air: The Invisible Powerhouse

Air is everywhere around you, even though you can't see it. It's a mix of gases, like oxygen and nitrogen, that we need to breathe. Without air, a lot of things wouldn't work, like fires, airplanes, or even your voice.

Fun Fact: The air we breathe is about 78% nitrogen and only 21% oxygen. That last 1% is other gases, like carbon dioxide.

Think About It: Air might not be alive, but it helps other things (like fire) thrive. Pretty important for something invisible!

Stars: The Giants of the Sky

Stars are massive balls of gas that shine because of nuclear reactions happening in their cores. They grow brighter as they burn through their fuel, and when they run out of energy, they either fade away or explode as supernovas.

Fun Fact: Our Sun is a star, and it's about halfway through its life. It's got another 5 billion years before it burns out.

You're Made of Stardust

That's right—you're basically a walking, talking piece of the universe. The carbon, oxygen, and other elements in your body were created inside stars billions of years ago. When those stars exploded, they scattered their stardust across the galaxy.

Fun Fact: The iron in your blood and the calcium in your bones? Yep, all stardust. So, the next time someone calls you special, just say, "Of course—I'm made of stars!"

Earth Has More Than One "Moon"

Okay, Earth doesn't really have extra moons like in a sci-fi movie, but there are some big space rocks, called *quasi-satellites*, that follow Earth's orbit around the Sun. They're like the Moon's shy little cousins.

Fun Fact: One of these rocks, called 3753 Cruithne, is sometimes nicknamed "Earth's second moon," even though it's not a true moon. Still pretty cool, right?

Spiders Can Fly

Spiders don't just crawl—they can also "fly" by using a process called *ballooning*. They release tiny silk threads that catch the wind, lifting them up and carrying them miles away. It's like a parachute, but way cooler.

Fun Fact: Scientists have found spiders floating as high as 2.5 miles above the ground. Spiderman, eat your heart out!

A Day on Venus is Longer Than a Year

Venus is the slowpoke of the solar system. It takes 243 Earth days for Venus to complete one rotation (one day), but it only takes 225 Earth days to orbit the Sun (one year). That means you'd celebrate your birthday before bedtime on Venus!

Fun Fact: Venus also spins *backward* compared to most other planets. It's like the rebel of the solar system.

Slime Mold is Smarter Than You Think

Slime mold might sound gross, but it's actually kind of a genius. This gooey organism can solve mazes, find the shortest path to food, and even mimic the efficiency of subway systems—all without a brain!

Fun Fact: Scientists once used slime mold to design a transportation map for Tokyo, and it worked surprisingly well. Who knew slime could be so smart?

Your Heart Beats Over 100,000 Times a Day

Your heart is like the Energizer Bunny—it keeps going and going. In just one day, your heart pumps enough blood to fill about 50 bathtubs.

Fun Fact: Your heart works so hard that over a lifetime, it could pump enough blood to fill a swimming pool the size of an Olympic stadium!

Water Can Boil and Freeze at the Same Time

This mind-blowing phenomenon is called the *triple point*. It happens when water is at just the right temperature and pressure to exist as a solid, liquid, and gas all at once.

Where It Happens: In a science lab or outer space. You won't see this happening in your kitchen anytime soon!

Fun Fact: Scientists use the triple point of water to help define the Kelvin temperature scale.

The Ocean Is Full of Gold

If you've ever dreamed of being a treasure hunter, the ocean is the place to go. There's about 20 million tons of gold dissolved in seawater. Unfortunately, it's spread out over such a huge area that it's almost impossible to collect.

Fun Fact: If all the gold in the ocean were evenly distributed, everyone on Earth would get about 9 pounds of gold. Time to dive in!

The Smallest Thing You Can See Is... Huge

The smallest thing your eyes can see without help is about 0.1 millimeters wide. That's about the size of a human hair. But in the world of atoms and molecules, that's gigantic! Atoms are so small that millions of them could fit on the tip of a pencil.

Fun Fact: If an atom were the size of a football stadium, its nucleus would be the size of a pea.

The Speed of a Sneeze

When you sneeze, your body doesn't mess around. A sneeze can shoot out of your nose at speeds of up to 100 miles per hour. That's faster than most sports cars!

Fun Fact: Sneezes can send about 100,000 tiny droplets flying through the air. (So, cover your mouth!)

Bananas Are Radioactive

Bananas contain potassium-40, a radioactive isotope of potassium. Don't worry, though—it's totally safe to eat bananas. You'd have to eat about 10 million bananas at once to get a dangerous dose of radiation.

Fun Fact: Scientists use the term "banana equivalent dose" to compare radiation levels. Eating a banana equals about 0.1 microsieverts of radiation.

Trees "Talk" to Each Other

Through underground networks of fungi, trees can share nutrients, send warnings about pests, and even help each other grow. Scientists call it the "wood wide web."

Fun Fact: Some older trees, called "mother trees," are like community hubs, helping younger trees survive and thrive.

Octopuses Have Three Hearts

Not one, not two, but THREE hearts! Two pump blood to the octopus's gills, and one pumps it to the rest of the body. And here's the twist: the heart that pumps to the body stops beating when the octopus swims.

Fun Fact: Octopus blood is blue because it's rich in copper, not iron like ours. That makes them super unique—and super cool.

You wake up in the morning, heat your breakfast in the microwave, flip on a light, maybe scroll on a tablet, and never think twice about *how* all that magic happens. But here's a secret, your everyday gadgets aren't magic— they're powered by some seriously cool science. Let's peel back the curtain and figure out how these everyday things work.

How Microwaves Cook Your Food

Microwaves are like tiny wizards hiding in your kitchen. You pop in your leftovers, hit a button, and boom—warm food in minutes. But what's really happening in there?

Microwaves use… well, microwaves! Not the oven itself, but invisible waves of energy. These waves bounce around inside and make water molecules in your food wiggle really fast. The wiggling creates heat, and just like that, your pizza is warm again!

Cool Fact: The invention of the microwave was an accident! A scientist named Percy Spencer was working on radar technology when he noticed the chocolate bar in his pocket melted. Instead of getting mad about his messy pants, he thought, "Hey, I could cook stuff with this!"

How Light Bulbs Work

Flick! The room goes from dark and spooky to bright and cozy. But how does a light bulb actually work?

There are different types of light bulbs, but the classic kind—incandescent bulbs—work like this:

1.   Electricity flows through a super-thin wire inside the bulb, called a filament.

2.   The filament gets so hot that it glows. (Yep, the light you see is actually *super hot wire!*)

3.   The glass around the filament keeps it from burning up in the air.

37

LED bulbs, which are more common now, are even cooler—they create light using tiny semiconductors instead of heat.

Fun Fact: Thomas Edison is famous for inventing the light bulb, but dozens of other scientists helped make it possible. Teamwork makes the dream work!

How Wi-Fi Connects Everything

Wi-Fi is like the invisible magic carpet of the internet. It sends information back and forth between your devices and the internet *without any wires*. But how does it do that? Here's the secret: Wi-Fi uses radio waves. These waves carry information (like your favorite YouTube videos) from a router to your devices. The router acts like a tiny traffic cop, making sure all your gadgets get the data they need.

Fun Fact: Wi-Fi stands for "Wireless Fidelity," which is just a fancy way of saying "internet without the cords."

How Elevators Go Up and Down

Ever wondered how elevators make moving between floors look so easy? It's all about cables, pulleys, and counterweights.

1.	When you press a button, an electric motor pulls on a steel cable connected to the elevator.

2.	A counterweight moves in the opposite direction to balance everything out. (Think of it like a giant teeter-totter.)

3.	The motor controls how fast the elevator moves and makes sure it stops right where it's supposed to.

Fun Fact: Modern elevators are so safe that even if the cables broke (which almost never happens), built-in brakes would stop the elevator from falling. Phew!

How Airplanes Fly

Planes are giant, heavy machines, so how on Earth do they stay in the sky? It's all thanks to a little thing called **lift.**

1.	When a plane's engines push it forward, air moves over the wings.

2.	The wings are designed so that air moves faster over the top than the bottom.

3.	Faster air creates lower pressure, which lifts the plane up—like a giant invisible hand holding it in the sky.

Fun Fact: The Wright brothers invented the first airplane in 1903. Their first flight lasted only 12 seconds, but it changed the world forever.

How Fridges Keep Food Cold

Your fridge is like a superhero protecting your milk, veggies, and leftovers from spoiling. But instead of wearing a cape, it uses a clever cycle of heat and cold.

1.   Inside your fridge, there's a liquid called refrigerant.

2.   The refrigerant absorbs heat from inside the fridge, making it cold.

3.   Then, it carries the heat outside to the back of the fridge, where it releases it.

This cycle happens over and over, keeping your food fresh and tasty.

Fun Fact: Before fridges were invented, people used ice boxes filled with giant blocks of ice to keep food cool. Talk about a workout for the delivery guy!

How Batteries Work

Without batteries, we wouldn't have phones, remote controls, or even flashlights. But what's going on inside that little cylinder?

Batteries store energy in the form of chemicals. When you pop one into a device, a chemical reaction happens inside, creating electricity. That electricity powers your gadget until the chemicals run out.

Fun Fact: The first battery was invented in 1800 by Alessandro Volta. That's why we measure electricity in volts—named after him!

How GPS Finds Your Location

Ever used a GPS to figure out where you are? It's like having an all-knowing guide in your pocket. But how does it know where you are?

GPS (Global Positioning System) uses satellites in space. These satellites send signals to your device, telling it how far away they are. By combining signals from several satellites, your GPS figures out your exact location.

Fun Fact: There are at least 31 GPS satellites orbiting Earth right now, making sure you never get lost.

How Traffic Lights Know When to Change

Have you ever wondered how traffic lights seem to know when cars are waiting? Are there tiny elves inside pressing buttons? Nope—it's all about sensors and timers.

1. **Sensors:** Many traffic lights have sensors buried under the road. When a car drives over the sensor, it sends a signal to the traffic light saying, "Hey, I'm here!"

2. **Timers:** Other lights just use timers. They change at set intervals, like every 60 seconds.

3.   **Smart Systems:** In some cities, traffic lights are part of a big network that adjusts based on how much traffic there is.

Fun Fact: Some traffic lights use cameras to detect cars, so don't try to sneak through a red light. The camera's got your number!

How Toilets Flush

The humble toilet is one of the most important inventions in history. But how does it work? Let's flush out the details!

1.   When you press the handle, it lifts a rubber flap inside the toilet tank.

2.   Water from the tank rushes into the bowl, creating a whirlpool that washes everything away.

3.   Gravity does the rest, sending the waste down a pipe and into the sewer.

Fun Fact: The modern toilet was invented in 1596 by Sir John Harington, but it didn't become popular until much later. Imagine life without it—yikes!

How Touchscreens Work

You tap, swipe, and zoom on your phone or tablet without even thinking about it. But how does the screen know what you want it to do?

1.   **Electricity:** Touchscreens have a special layer that detects the tiny electric charge from your fingertip.

2.   **Coordinates:** When you touch the screen, it figures out the exact spot where you tapped.

3.   **Action:** The device uses this information to perform the action you asked for—like opening an app or playing a game.

Fun Fact: If you wear gloves, your screen might not work because it can't detect your fingertip's electric charge. That's why special touchscreen gloves exist!

How Zippers Zip

Zippers are simple but brilliant. They turn two separate pieces of fabric into one. Here's how they work:

1.   Zippers have two rows of tiny teeth.

2.   When you pull the slider, it pushes the teeth together, locking them in place.

3.   Pull the slider the other way, and the teeth unlock, opening the zipper.

Fun Fact: The modern zipper was invented in 1913 by Gideon Sundback, and it was originally called a "hookless fastener." Not as catchy as "zipper," huh?

How Ice Cream Machines Make Your Favorite Treat

Ice cream machines are like magic wands for dessert lovers, but it's all science:

1.   The machine keeps the mixture really cold while stirring it.

2.   The stirring adds air, which makes the ice cream fluffy.

3.   When it's ready, you get a creamy, delicious treat. Yum!

Fun Fact: The first ice cream machine was invented in 1843 by Nancy Johnson, and it was powered by hand-cranking—no electricity required!

How Vacuum Cleaners Suck (In a Good Way!)

Vacuum cleaners are like your home's superheroes, swooping in to clean up crumbs, dirt, and dust. But how do they work?

1.   **Fan Power:** A vacuum cleaner has a fan that creates suction.

2.   **Air Pressure:** The suction lowers the air pressure inside the vacuum, which pulls dirt and debris into it.

3.   **Filter:** The dirt gets trapped in a bag or filter, leaving clean air to flow out.

Fun Fact: The first vacuum cleaner was so big it had to be pulled by horses! Imagine cleaning your room with that.

How Balloons Float

Have you ever wondered why some balloons stay on the ground while others float up, up, and away? It's all about what's inside them.

1.   Balloons filled with helium (a super-light gas) are lighter than the air around them, so they float.

2.   Balloons filled with regular air are heavier than the surrounding air, so they stay on the ground.

Fun Fact: Helium is the second-lightest element in the universe, right after hydrogen. That's why it makes your voice sound so funny when you breathe it in!

How Clocks Keep Time

Tick-tock—how do clocks manage to keep track of every second of the day?

1.   **Quartz Clocks:** These use a tiny piece of quartz crystal that vibrates at a super steady rate when electricity passes through it.

2.   **Mechanical Clocks:** Gears and springs inside the clockwork together to measure time.

3.   **Atomic Clocks:** The most accurate clocks in the world use the vibrations of atoms to keep time. They're so precise they won't lose a second for millions of years!

Fun Fact: Atomic clocks are used in GPS systems to make sure they're accurate down to the millisecond.

How Your Voice Travels on the Phone

Ever thought about how your voice travels through a phone? It's not magic—it's technology!

1.   **Microphone:** Your phone's microphone turns the sound of your voice into an electrical signal.

2.   **Signal:** That signal gets sent through wires or the air to the person on the other end.

3.   **Speaker:** The signal turns back into sound in their phone's speaker. Voila!

Fun Fact: The first phone call was made in 1876 by Alexander Graham Bell, who said, "Mr. Watson, come here—I want to see you." (Not exactly "Hello, world!" but hey, it was a start.)

The coolest part about knowing how stuff works is that it makes the world around you feel like a giant puzzle you can figure out. Who knows? Maybe one day you'll invent a gadget that makes life even better—like a teleporting backpack or a snack-making robot!

Keep exploring, stay curious, and remember: science is all around you.

The Amazing World of Kitchen Chemistry
Where Your Kitchen Becomes a Science Lab!

Did you know that right now, in your very own kitchen, there's a super-secret laboratory just waiting to be discovered? That's right! Those cabinets and drawers are packed with amazing chemicals (don't worry, they're just regular ingredients) that can help us learn about science in the most delicious and fun ways possible!

The Great Cabbage Mystery

Have you ever wondered how scientists figure out if something is an acid or a base? Well, get ready for this mind-blowing fact: You can make your own pH indicator using... wait for it... CABBAGE! Yes, that purple veggie your mom always tries to get you to eat can actually be turned into a magical color-changing potion!

Safe Kitchen Experiment #1: Rainbow Juice *What you'll need (ask a grown-up to help):*

- ★ 1/4 of a red cabbage
- ★ Hot water
- ★ White cups or clear glasses
- ★ Common kitchen items like lemon juice, baking soda, and vinegar

Steps:

1. Chop up the cabbage and put it in a bowl

2. Add hot water (careful - let an adult help!)

3. Wait until the water turns purple

4.   Strain out the cabbage pieces

5.   Pour your purple cabbage juice into different cups

6.   Add different kitchen items to each cup and watch the magic happen!

When you add lemon juice, your purple liquid turns pink! Add baking soda, and POOF - it's blue or green! It's like having your own magical chemistry set, except it's totally safe and made from stuff you can eat (though your cabbage juice probably won't taste very good 😁).

The Dancing Raisin Disco Party

Here's something wild: Did you know raisins can dance? No, they haven't been taking ballet lessons, but with this next experiment, you'll make them bust some moves!

Safe Kitchen Experiment #2: Dancing Raisins *What you'll need:*

- ★ Clear glass
- ★ Carbonated clear soda (like Sprite or club soda)
- ★ Raisins
- ★ Your best dance moves (optional, but recommended!)

Steps:

1.   Fill the glass with soda

2.   Drop in a few raisins

3.   Watch them dance!

The raisins will bob up and down like they're at the world's tiniest disco. But why? It's all because of BUBBLES! The carbonation (those tiny bubbles in the soda) sticks to the wrinkly surface of the raisins, making them float up. When the bubbles pop at the top, the raisins sink back down. It's like an endless elevator ride for dried grapes!

The Incredible Expanding Universe (of Bread)

Speaking of bubbles, did you know that every time someone bakes bread, they're actually doing a science experiment? Yeast (tiny living organisms) eat sugar and burp out carbon dioxide bubbles that make bread rise. Gross? Maybe. Cool? Definitely!

Safe Kitchen Experiment #3: Yeast Beast Feast *What you'll need:*

- ★ Empty clear plastic bottle
- ★ Balloon
- ★ Warm water
- ★ 1 packet of yeast
- ★ 1 teaspoon sugar

Steps:

1.   Fill the bottle with about 1 inch of warm water

2.   Add the yeast and sugar

3.   Stretch the balloon over the bottle top

4.   Wait and watch!

The balloon will slowly inflate as the yeast "burps" out carbon dioxide. It's like having a tiny pet monster that likes to blow up balloons! Just remember: this is exactly what happens inside bread dough, except the bubbles get trapped in the dough instead of filling up a balloon.

Did You Know?

★ A single teaspoon of yeast contains about 100 BILLION tiny yeast organisms! That's more than all the people on Earth!

★ The bubbles in soda can make a raisin travel up and down more than 100 times before running out of energy

★ Red cabbage has been used as a natural dye and pH indicator for hundreds of years

Make Your Own Lava Lamp

What You'll Need:

★ A clear bottle or jar

★ Water

★ Vegetable oil

★ Food coloring

★   Alka-Seltzer tablets

What to Do:

1.   Fill the bottle about 1/3 full with water.

2.   Add food coloring to the water.

3.   Pour vegetable oil into the bottle until it's nearly full. (Don't worry—oil and water don't mix!)

4.   Break an Alka-Seltzer tablet into pieces and drop them in one at a time.

5.   Watch as your lava lamp comes to life!

What's Going On?

The Alka-Seltzer creates bubbles of carbon dioxide gas. These bubbles lift the colored water through the oil, creating that awesome lava-lamp effect.

Safety Tip: Don't seal the bottle while the reaction is happening. Let the gas escape.

Magic Milk Art

What You'll Need:

★   A shallow dish

★   Milk (whole milk works best)

★   Food coloring

★   Dish soap

★   A cotton swab

What to Do:

1.   Pour the milk into the dish so it covers the bottom.

2.   Add a few drops of different food colors around the milk.

3.   Dip a cotton swab into dish soap and gently touch it to the milk.

4.   Watch the colors swirl and dance like magic!

What's Going On?

The dish soap breaks down the fat in the milk, causing the food coloring to swirl around. It's like a colorful science dance party!

Pro Tip: Try different types of milk to see if the results change.

The Balloon That Won't Pop

What You'll Need:

- ★ A balloon

- ★ A few pieces of tape

- ★ A sharp pin

What to Do:

1.   Blow up the balloon and tie it.

2.   Stick a small piece of tape on the balloon.

3.   Gently poke the pin through the tape. Surprise— the balloon won't pop!

What's Going On?

The tape holds the rubber tightly together, so when you poke it, the hole stays small and the air doesn't rush out. Without the tape, the rubber stretches too much and pops!

Fun Fact: Scientists use this concept to make special materials that can stretch without breaking.

Instant Ice!

What You'll Need:

* ★ A bottle of purified water
* ★ A freezer
* ★ A bowl

What to Do:

1. Place the bottle of water in the freezer for about 2 hours. Check it often—it should be super cold but not frozen solid.

2. Gently remove the bottle and pour the water into a bowl.

3. Watch as it instantly turns into ice before your eyes!

What's Going On?

The water was supercooled in the freezer, meaning it stayed liquid even though it was below its freezing point.

When you pour it out, the movement triggers the water to freeze instantly.

Safety Tip: Don't leave the water in the freezer too long, or it'll freeze solid and ruin the experiment.

Invisible Ink

What You'll Need:

★ Lemon juice

★ A cotton swab

★ Paper

★ A lamp or light bulb

What to Do:

1.   Dip the cotton swab into the lemon juice and use it to write a secret message on the paper.

2.   Let the paper dry completely.

3.   Hold the paper close to a lamp or light bulb (ask an adult to help with this part).

4.   Watch as your secret message appears!

What's Going On?

The heat from the lamp causes the lemon juice to oxidize, turning it brown and revealing your secret writing.

Fun Fact: People used invisible ink to send secret messages during wars and spy missions!

What You'll Need:

- ★ An egg
- ★ Vinegar
- ★ A glass or jar

What to Do:

1. Place the egg in the jar.

2. Pour vinegar over the egg until it's completely covered.

3. Leave it for 24-48 hours. Check back the next day to see what's happening.

4. Gently rinse the egg under water. Now, it's bouncy!

What's Going On?

The vinegar dissolves the eggshell, leaving the squishy membrane underneath. That's what makes it bouncy. Careful, though—it's still an egg and can break if you bounce it too hard!

The Big Question

Next time you're in the kitchen, look around and ask yourself: "What other science experiments are hiding in these cabinets?" Remember, some of the greatest scientific discoveries happened because someone got curious and tried something new (safely, of course!).

Always remember these super important rules:

1.   Get a grown-up's permission and help before trying any experiments

2.   Never eat or drink your experiments (even if they're made from food)

3.   Keep your lab (kitchen) clean and tidy

4.   Wear safety gear when needed (even if it's just an apron!)

Where Nature Throws the Most Amazing Party Ever!

Ready to discover some of the most jaw-dropping, mind-boggling, and totally real natural wonders on Earth? Buckle up, because we're about to explore places so amazing, you might think they came straight from a fairy tale — but they're 100% real!

The Ocean's Glow-in-the-Dark Party

Imagine walking along a beach at night when suddenly — WHOOSH! — every wave starts to glow bright blue! Sounds like magic, right? Well, this actually happens at certain beaches around the world, and it's all thanks to tiny organisms called dinoflagellates (try saying that three times fast! Dino-flag-eh-lates!).

Fun Fact Alert! These microscopic sea creatures are like billions of tiny living glow sticks! When the waves disturb them, they light up like Christmas trees underwater. It's their way of saying "Eek! Don't eat me!" to predators, but for us, it's nature's most amazing light show!

Where Can You See This?

★ Mosquito Bay, Puerto Rico (The brightest bio-bay in the world!)

★ Maldives Islands (Where the beach looks like a starry sky)

★ Tasmania, Australia (Where the waves glow electric blue)

DIY Glow Experiment (No Ocean Required!)

With adult supervision, try this safe version of bioluminescence:

1. Get a glow stick (the safe kind from the party store)

2. Fill a clear glass with water

3. Crack the glow stick and empty it into the water

4. Swish it around gently

5. Turn off the lights and watch your own mini glowing ocean!

Remember: This is just for fun — real bioluminescent organisms are much cooler because they're alive!

Nature's Light Show in the Sky: Aurora Borealis

You're standing in the snow, looking up at the night sky, when suddenly green, pink, and purple lights start dancing overhead! No, aliens aren't having a disco party (though that would be cool!) — it's the Northern Lights, or Aurora Borealis!

What's Really Happening Up There? The Sun shoots tiny particles into space (like a cosmic sneeze), and when these particles crash into Earth's magnetic shield, they create these amazing colorful lights! It's like nature's own laser light show, but way bigger and more spectacular.

Fun Fact: The Southern Hemisphere has its own version called Aurora Australis. Same light show, different hemisphere!

Why Different Colors?

★ Green: The most common color, caused by oxygen particles

★ Pink/Red: Nitrogen getting in on the party

★ Blue/Purple: When oxygen and nitrogen decide to dance together

★ Yellow/White: When all the colors mix together like a cosmic smoothie!

The Great Salt Desert Rainbow 🌈

Ever heard of a place where the ground looks like a giant rainbow? Welcome to Danxia Rainbow Mountains in China! These mountains look like someone took the biggest box of crayons ever and colored the rocks in stripes of red, yellow, green, and blue.

How Did They Get So Colorful? Millions of years ago, different types of rocks were layered on top of each other like a giant layer cake. Each layer had different minerals that created different colors:

- Red rocks: Iron (like rust!)
- Yellow: Sulfur (smells like rotten eggs – yuck!)
- Green: Copper (like the Statue of Liberty!)
- Blue: Cobalt (not the same as the blue crayon in your box!)

Make Your Own Rainbow Mountain!

Try this safe experiment at home:

1. Get different colored sand or salt (food coloring + salt works too!)
2. Layer them in a clear jar

3.   Don't shake it! Just watch how the layers form like real rock layers

4.   Congratulations! You're now a mini-geologist!

★ Some beaches in the Maldives glow so bright at night, you can read a book by their light!

★ The Northern Lights can make weird sounds like crackles and swooshes

★ There's a beach in Japan that glows blue all year round because of special algae

Your Mission (Should You Choose to Accept It)

Next time you're outside at night, look up at the sky. You never know – you might catch nature putting on one of its amazing light shows! And if you're near a beach, bring a grown-up and visit at night (safely!) to see if you can spot any glowing waves.

Safety First, Explorers!

★ Never go to the beach at night without an adult

★ Stay warm when watching the Northern Lights (they appear in cold places!)

★ Don't touch glowing creatures in the ocean (look, don't touch!)

★ Always bring a flashlight for nighttime adventures

Sailing Rocks: The Mystery of Moving Stones

In California's Death Valley, there's a place called Racetrack Playa where rocks move across the desert floor, leaving long trails behind them. But here's the weird part: no one sees them move!

What's Happening?

For years, scientists had no idea how the rocks slid around. Then they discovered that when it rains, the ground turns to slippery mud. A little wind and ice do the rest, pushing the rocks across the desert. Mystery solved!

Fun Fact: Some of these rocks weigh hundreds of pounds. Even nature's got a gym membership, apparently.

Blood Falls: A Red Waterfall in Antarctica

Antarctica is home to one of the strangest sights on Earth: a blood-red waterfall. Don't worry, it's not actual blood—it just looks like it!

What's Happening?

The water comes from a salty underground lake that's full of iron. When the iron hits the air, it rusts, turning the water red. It's like a spooky science experiment frozen in time.

Fun Fact: Blood Falls has been flowing for over a million years. That's one very determined waterfall!

The Great Blue Hole: An Underwater Sinkhole

Off the coast of Belize, there's a giant, perfectly round hole in the ocean called the Great Blue Hole. It's over 400 feet deep, and it looks like someone punched a hole in the Earth's surface.

What's Happening?

The Great Blue Hole formed thousands of years ago when an ancient cave collapsed. Now, it's a scuba diver's dream, full of colorful fish, stalactites, and mystery.

Fun Fact: The Great Blue Hole is so big that astronauts can see it from space!

Ice Circles: Nature's Spinning Discs

In cold rivers and lakes, you might spot giant spinning circles of ice. They look like nature's version of a record player, but what's going on here?

What's Happening?

When cold water flows in just the right way, it causes ice chunks to rotate and form perfect circles. They're rare, but when you see one, it's like Earth is showing off its geometry skills.

Fun Fact: Some ice circles can grow to over 50 feet wide. That's bigger than most swimming pools!

Morning Glory Clouds: Sky Rolls

In parts of Australia, the sky sometimes forms enormous, rolling clouds that look like giant white tubes stretching across the horizon. They're called Morning Glory clouds, and they're as rare as they are stunning.

What's Happening?

They form when warm air rises and meets cool air, creating a rolling effect. Pilots love flying through them because they create smooth, natural turbulence.

Fun Fact: Some Morning Glory clouds stretch for over 600 miles! That's longer than a trip from New York to Chicago.

Mud Volcanoes: Burping Earth

Imagine a volcano, but instead of spewing lava, it burps out mud. Mud volcanoes exist in places like Azerbaijan, and they're messy, weird, and totally fascinating.

What's Happening?

Gas and water trapped underground push mud to the surface, creating bubbly mud pools. Sometimes, the mud even catches fire because of the gas!

Fun Fact: Azerbaijan is called the "Land of Fire" because of its fiery mud volcanoes.

65

Fire Rainbows: Flames in the Sky

Fire rainbows aren't rainbows made of fire (although that would be cool). They're colorful arcs of light that appear in the sky and look like they're on fire.

What's Happening?

These rare rainbows form when sunlight hits ice crystals in the atmosphere at just the right angle. It's like nature playing with prisms!

Fun Fact: Fire rainbows can only happen when the Sun is high in the sky—so they're most common in summer.

Ever wondered where Earth keeps its most mind-blowing places? You know, the spots that make you say "NO WAY!" and "Is that even possible?!" Well, get ready, because we're about to visit places so extreme, they'll make your local weather forecast look boring!

The Ultimate Hot Spot: Death Valley 🌡️

Location: California, USA **Claim to Fame:** Hottest Place on Earth!

Imagine it's a hot summer day, and you're complaining about the heat. Now imagine it being SO hot that you could literally fry an egg on the sidewalk! That's Death

66

Valley for you, where the temperature once reached a whopping 134°F (56.7°C)!

Fun Fact: It's so hot here that sometimes your shoes might start melting if you stand in one place too long. Talk about a hot dance floor!

Safe Heat Experiment: *With adult supervision, try this:*

1.   Put a chocolate bar in three places:

   ★   In the shade

   ★   In the sun

   ★   On a plate in the sun

2.   Time how long it takes to melt in each spot

3.   Imagine being in Death Valley where it's WAY

hotter! (Bonus: You get to eat the chocolate afterward! ☺)

The Big Chill: Vostok Station, Antarctica

Location: Antarctica **Claim to Fame:** Coldest Place on Earth!

Think your freezer is cold? Ha! That's nothing compared to Vostok Station, where temperatures have dropped to -128.6°F (-89.2°C)! That's so cold that if you threw hot water into the air, it would turn into snow before hitting the ground!

Fun Fact: It's so cold here that scientists have to wear special masks because their breath would freeze on their faces! Talk about having ice on your face without trying the latest TikTok challenge!

Mount Everest: The World's Highest Traffic Jam 🏔️

Location: Nepal/Tibet border **Claim to Fame:** Tallest Mountain on Earth!

Standing at 29,029 feet (8,848 meters), Mount Everest is like a 2,000-story building made of rock and ice! It's so tall that:

- ★ Airplanes have to fly around it
- ★ The top has only 1/3 of the oxygen we breathe at sea level
- ★ Clouds look up to it (literally!)

Fun Fact: Everest grows about 4 millimeters (0.16 inches) taller every year! It's like a teenager going through a growth spurt, but REALLY slowly.

The Mariana Trench: Earth's Deepest Dimple 🌊

Location: Pacific Ocean **Claim to Fame:** Deepest Place on Earth!

Imagine taking 11 Mount Everests, stacking them upside down, and dropping them into the ocean — that's how deep the Mariana Trench is! At 36,070 feet (10,994 meters) deep, it's like nature's ultimate swimming pool, except:

★ The pressure is so strong it could crush a submarine like a soda can

★ It's darker than your room at night with ALL the lights off

★ Strange glowing creatures live down there that look like they're from another planet!

Try This: Make Your Own Pressure Test!

Safe experiment to understand deep-sea pressure:

1. Get a plastic bottle with a lid

2. Make a few small holes in it

3. Fill it with water

4. Squeeze! The harder you squeeze, the faster the water shoots out

5. Now imagine pressure so strong it could flatten your bottle completely!

Other EXTREME Places That'll Blow Your Mind

Dallol, Ethiopia: The Most Colorful Nightmare

★ Toxic gases ✓

★ Acid pools ✓

★ Rainbow-colored hot springs ✓

It's like Mother Nature went crazy with a paint set, but everything can hurt you!

Mount Thor, Canada: The World's Largest Cliff

- ★ 4,101-foot (1,250-meter) vertical drop
- ★ If you dropped a penny from the top, it would take 7 seconds to hit bottom!
- ★ Rock climbers call it "the ultimate challenge" (we call it "the ultimate NOPE!")

Did You Know?

- ★ The temperature difference between Earth's hottest and coldest places is bigger than the difference between freezing and boiling water!
- ★ If Mount Everest were placed in the Mariana Trench, its peak would still be about a mile underwater!
- ★ Death Valley is so hot that rangers can cook cookies on their car dashboards (probably not very tasty though)

Safety Corner (Because We Care!)

Remember:

- ★ Never try to visit extreme places without proper preparation and adult supervision
- ★ Most of these places are dangerous and require special training to visit
- ★ Stay safe by learning about them from books (like this one!) and documentaries

Next time someone complains about the weather being too hot or too cold, share these extreme facts with them! Watch their jaw drop when they realize their "too hot" is nothing compared to Death Valley's "egg-frying" temperatures!

Quick Quiz!

1.   What would happen to a snowball in Death Valley? (Hint: It wouldn't last long enough for a snowball fight!)

2.   How many Empire State Buildings could you stack in the Mariana Trench? (Get ready for some big numbers!)

3.   Why don't commercial airplanes fly over Mount Everest? (Besides being scared of heights!)

Weather is something we deal with every day. Sometimes it's sunny, sometimes it rains, and sometimes the weatherman says it'll snow but you still have school anyway (ugh). But did you know that weather can get really, really weird? Like *raining fish* kind of weird? Or *purple lightning* kind of weird?

1. Raining Animals: When the Sky Goes Wild

Yep, you read that right. In some places, it rains frogs, fish, or even spiders. This isn't a prank—this is Mother Nature showing off her sense of humor.

72

Where It Happens:

- ★ Honduras has an event called "Lluvia de Peces," or "Rain of Fish." It happens every year after heavy rainstorms.

- ★ In Australia, there have been reports of frogs falling from the sky.

What's Going On?

Strong winds, like tornadoes or waterspouts (mini tornadoes over water), suck up animals from rivers or lakes and carry them into the sky. When the winds lose power, the animals fall back down. Imagine walking outside and being bonked on the head by a fish!

Fun Fact: Don't worry—this doesn't happen everywhere, so your umbrella is still mostly for rain.

2. Glowing Skies: Nature's Nightlight

Sometimes, the sky lights up in ways that seem straight out of a sci-fi movie. From purple lightning to eerie green glows, weird skies are nature's version of a rave.

- ★ **Purple Lightning:** This happens during powerful storms when rain, wind, and clouds interact in just the right way. It's rare and super cool!

★ **Green Skies Before Tornadoes:** If the sky turns green, it's often a warning sign that a tornado might be nearby.

What's Going On?

Green skies happen when sunlight filters through storm clouds filled with water and hail. Purple lightning? That's just Mother Nature adding flair to her thunderstorm.

Fun Fact: Green skies don't guarantee a tornado, but they definitely make you pay attention.

3. Ball Lightning: The Floating Fireball

Imagine a glowing orb of light floating through the air during a thunderstorm. Sounds like something from a wizard movie, right? Nope—it's ball lightning, one of the weirdest and rarest weather phenomena.

What's Going On?

Scientists still don't know exactly how ball lightning forms, but they think it might be caused by electricity interacting with the air. The glowing ball can float, bounce, and even pass through windows before disappearing with a bang. Spooky!

Fun Fact: Ball lightning is so rare that some people thought it was a myth—until scientists captured it on camera.

4. Blood Rain: When the Sky Cries Red

If red rain started falling from the sky, you'd probably think, *"Is this the end of the world?"* Relax—it's not! Blood rain is a real thing, and it's not as scary as it sounds.

Where It Happens:

★ India, Sri Lanka, and parts of Europe have all reported red rain.

What's Going On?

Tiny particles of red dust or algae get mixed into rain clouds, turning the raindrops red. It's completely natural, but it looks like something out of a spooky movie.

Fun Fact: The red rain in Kerala, India, turned out to be caused by a harmless type of algae. Crisis averted!

5. Ice Bombs: Winter's Surprise Attack

Imagine walking outside on a sunny day and being hit by a chunk of ice that fell from the sky. Ice bombs are exactly that—giant chunks of ice that fall out of nowhere.

What's Going On?

Ice bombs form when water vapor in the atmosphere freezes into large chunks. Sometimes, they break off from planes flying overhead, but other times, they seem to come from nowhere.

Fun Fact: These ice chunks can weigh as much as a bowling ball. That's one way to ruin a picnic!

6. Fire Tornadoes: When Tornadoes Get Even Scarier

What's scarier than a regular tornado? A *fire tornado*. These happen when hot, dry conditions combine with strong winds to create a spinning vortex of flames.

Where It Happens:

★ Fire tornadoes are most common during wildfires in places like California or Australia.

What's Going On?

The intense heat from a wildfire creates rising air currents, which spin into a fiery vortex. It's like a tornado decided to take fire along for the ride.

Fun Fact: Fire tornadoes can reach temperatures of over 2,000°F. That's hotter than most pizza ovens!

7. Snow Donuts: Winter's Weirdest Trick

Snow isn't just for building snowmen—it can also make donuts. Snow donuts (or snow rollers) are rare, naturally formed rings of snow that look like perfect pastry wheels.

What's Going On?

Strong winds blow loose snow across the ground, causing it to roll into hollow cylinders. They're super fragile and can collapse if touched, so no eating these donuts!

Fun Fact: Snow donuts can grow as big as a car tire, but most are smaller.

8. The Everlasting Storm: Earth's Lightning Capital

In Venezuela, there's a place called Lake Maracaibo where lightning strikes nearly every night. This stormy area, called the Catatumbo Lightning, sees up to 280 strikes per hour!

What's Going On?

Warm air from the lake meets cool mountain air, creating perfect conditions for non-stop lightning. It's so consistent that sailors once used it as a natural lighthouse.

Fun Fact: The Catatumbo Lightning is so famous, it's even on Venezuela's flag.

9. The Mysterious Fog Bows

You know rainbows, but have you ever seen a fog bow? These white, ghostly arcs appear when sunlight passes through fog instead of rain.

What's Going On?

Fog droplets are much smaller than raindrops, so instead of colorful rainbows, they create pale, glowing bows.

Fun Fact: Fog bows are sometimes called "white rainbows" or "ghost rainbows."

10. Frozen Waves: When Water Stops Mid-Crash

In super-cold places like Antarctica, waves can freeze while they're still crashing. It's like someone hit the pause button on the ocean.

What's Going On?

Freezing temperatures turn the water into solid ice before the wave can finish falling. The result? An icy masterpiece that looks like it's straight out of a fantasy movie.

Fun Fact: Frozen waves can stay in place for weeks until they finally melt.

Chapter 2

Geography and Earth Wonders

Fascinating Facts About Different Cultures
and Traditions

People everywhere have unique ways of celebrating, eating, and even saying hello. Some are heartwarming, some are hilarious, and all of them are fascinating. Let's pack our imaginary suitcases and take a trip through the incredible customs and traditions that make our planet so awesome!

1. Greeting People: Not Everyone Shakes Hands

79

In some places, shaking hands is the go-to way to say hello, but around the world, greetings get a lot more creative.

* **New Zealand:** The Māori people greet each other with the *hongi,* where they press their noses together. It's like saying, "Let's share a breath."

* **Tibet:** Some people in Tibet stick out their tongues to greet others. Don't worry—it's not rude. It's their way of showing respect!

* **Japan:** People bow to say hello. The deeper the bow, the more respect you're showing.

Fun Fact: In the Philippines, kids often take an elder's hand and press it to their forehead as a sign of respect. It's called *mano po.*

2. Food Traditions: Meals Are More Than Just Eating

What's on the menu? Around the world, food isn't just about filling your belly—it's full of meaning and celebration!

* **India:** Eating with your hands is common (and fun!). It's believed that eating this way helps you connect with the food.

- ★ **Mexico:** Tacos are eaten with tortillas as utensils. If you try to use a fork and knife, you might get a funny look.
- ★ **China:** During Chinese New Year, families eat dumplings because they look like gold ingots, symbolizing wealth and good fortune.

Fun Fact: In Ethiopia, meals are often shared from a single large plate. Using your right hand, you scoop up food with flatbread called injera.

3. Festivals: The World Knows How to Celebrate

Festivals are like a country's way of saying, "Let's party!" But not all parties are the same.

- ★ **India:** Holi, the Festival of Colors, is a giant, joyful paint fight. People throw bright powders at each other to celebrate the arrival of spring.
- ★ **Thailand:** Songkran is a New Year celebration where people have water fights in the streets. Getting splashed is part of the fun.

Fun Fact: In Japan, during Hanami season, people have picnics under blooming cherry trees to celebrate the beauty of nature.

4. Unique Homes: Living Spaces from Around the World

Where people live can be as fascinating as how they live.

★ **Mongolia:** Many families live in *gers* (or yurts), which are round, portable tents. They're cozy and perfect for nomadic lifestyles.

★ **Italy:** In the city of Matera, some homes are carved into cliffs and caves. They're called *sassi,* and people have lived in them for thousands of years.

★ **The Arctic:** Some Inuit people build igloos out of snow to stay warm. Snow might seem cold, but it's actually a great insulator.

Fun Fact: In Bolivia, you can stay in a hotel made entirely of salt, including the walls, beds, and even the chairs! Just don't lick the furniture.

5. Clothing: What You Wear Tells a Story

Clothing isn't just about looking good—it can also represent history, culture, and tradition.

★ **Scotland:** Men wear kilts made of tartan, a pattern that represents their family or clan.

★ **India:** Women often wear sarees, long pieces of fabric draped elegantly around the body.

★ **Japan:** Traditional kimonos are worn for special occasions and are often decorated with beautiful patterns.

Fun Fact: In Kenya and Tanzania, the Maasai people wear brightly colored clothing called *shukas*. Red is a favorite color because it represents bravery.

6. Fun Superstitions: Beliefs That Might Surprise You

Superstitions are fun (and sometimes a little silly) beliefs about good and bad luck. Here are some interesting ones:

★ **Russia:** Whistling indoors is thought to bring bad luck or financial trouble.

★ **South Korea:** Some people believe sleeping with a fan on in a closed room can be dangerous. It's called "fan death."

★ **Turkey:** Spilling water behind someone as they leave is considered good luck. It means they'll have a smooth journey.

Fun Fact: In many parts of the world, finding a four-leaf clover is considered super lucky. Start searching in your backyard!

7. Weddings: Tying the Knot with Style

Weddings are full of traditions, and each culture has its own unique way of celebrating love.

- ★ **India:** Brides often have their hands and feet decorated with intricate henna designs.
- ★ **Germany:** Guests at some weddings smash dishes to bring good luck, and the couple has to clean it up together.
- ★ **Mexico:** A *lazo,* or large loop of ribbon, is placed around the couple to symbolize their union.

Fun Fact: In Kenya, the Maasai bless newlyweds by spitting on them! Don't worry—it's meant to bring good fortune, not gross them out.

8. Saying Goodbye: Traditions for Farewells

Goodbyes are just as important as hellos, and cultures have creative ways of parting ways.

- ★ **France:** People say goodbye with a cheek kiss—one, two, or even three times, depending on the region.
- ★ **Japan:** Bowing deeply shows respect when saying goodbye.
- ★ **Italy:** The phrase "Arrivederci" means "until we see each other again," which sounds so much nicer than just "goodbye."

Fun Fact: In some Pacific Island cultures, people wave with both hands as a sign of extra friendliness.

The Great Spanish Food Fight! 🍅

Ever been told not to play with your food? Well, in the town of Buñol, Spain, they have a whole festival dedicated to throwing tomatoes at each other! It's called La Tomatina, and it turns the entire town into the world's biggest food fight!

Fun Fact: They use about 150,000 tomatoes during the festival. That's enough to make spaghetti sauce for an entire city!

Try This at Home (The Clean Version!): Make your own festival colors with this safe activity:

1.   Get some washable paint

2.   Dip your hands in different colors

3.   Make hand prints on paper

4.   Create your own festival artwork!

(Remember: No throwing paint or food at anyone!)

The Walking Houses of Japan 🏠

In Japan, when people need to move their traditional wooden houses, they don't always use trucks. Sometimes, they get the whole neighborhood together to CARRY the house! It's called "Yatai" moving, and it looks like a giant game of house-lifting!

How They Do It:

1. Everyone grabs long wooden poles
2. They slide the poles under the house
3. On the count of three... LIFT!
4. The whole house moves like it's taking a walk!

The Tooth Fairy's Global Cousins

Think the Tooth Fairy is the only one collecting teeth? Think again! Around the world, kids have different traditions for their lost teeth:

- ★ In Spain: A mouse called Pérez collects teeth
- ★ In Japan: Kids throw their teeth straight up (upper teeth) or straight down (lower teeth)
- ★ In Turkey: Parents bury baby teeth in a place that will help their child's future career (like a soccer field if they want to be an athlete!)

The World's Most Colorful Celebrations 🎨

India's Holi Festival Imagine a party where everyone throws colored powder at each other until everyone looks like a living rainbow! That's Holi for you! It celebrates:

- ★ The victory of good over evil
- ★ The arrival of spring

★ The joy of making everyone look silly with colors!

Thailand's Water Festival During Songkran, the entire country has a giant water fight! But it's not just for fun - it's about:

★ Washing away bad luck

★ Blessing others with good fortune

★ Getting totally soaked in the process!

Weird and Wonderful Birthday Traditions 🎂

Denmark's Surprise Attack In Denmark, if you're not married by your 25th birthday, your friends might cover you in cinnamon! (Yes, the same stuff you put on cookies!)

South Korea's Special Noodles On birthdays, Koreans eat super long noodles called "janchi guksu" - the longer the noodle, the longer your life will be!

Make Your Own Tradition!

Every tradition started somewhere! Here's how to create your own:

1. Think of something that makes you happy

2. Create a special way to celebrate it

3. Share it with your family and friends

4. Keep doing it until it becomes a tradition!

Did You Know?

- ★ In Ethiopia, some tribes tell time by cooking coffee! Each coffee ceremony takes about 3 hours
- ★ In Tibet, sticking out your tongue is a polite greeting
- ★ In New Zealand, Māori warriors greet each other by pressing their noses together (it's called "hongi")

The World's Weirdest Table Manners

- ★ In Japan: Slurping your noodles loudly is good manners - it shows you're enjoying the food!
- ★ In India: Eating with your hands is normal and traditional
- ★ In China: Leaving a little food on your plate shows you're full (in other places, it's considered rude!)

Try This: Global Greetings Game!

Learn how people say hello around the world:

- ★ Japan: Bow from the waist
- ★ France: Kiss on both cheeks
- ★ Thailand: Press your hands together and bow slightly
- ★ Māori: Press noses and foreheads together

Practice these with your family (but maybe skip the cinnamon throwing! ☺)

Fun With Food Traditions

Safe Kitchen Activity: Make a simple international snack:

★ Japanese Rice Balls (Onigiri):

1. Cook some rice

2. Wet your hands

3. Shape rice into triangles

4. Wrap with seaweed (Always ask a grown-up to help in the kitchen!)

Cultural Respect Corner

Remember:

★ Every tradition is special to someone

★ Different isn't weird - it's wonderful!

★ Learning about other cultures makes us smarter and kinder

★ Always be respectful when learning about other traditions

Your Global Mission

1. Learn to say "hello" in three new languages

2. Try a food from another culture (with parent's permission!)

3. Share something cool about your own culture with a friend

Quick Quiz Time!

1.   Why do people throw tomatoes in Spain?

2.   What happens to lost teeth in Japan?

3.   What's special about birthday noodles in Korea? (Answers are hiding somewhere in your parent's sock drawer... just kidding, they're in this book!)

It's Party Time

Everyone loves a good birthday party, but the way people celebrate can be wildly different depending on where you live.

- ★ **Mexico:** Ever heard of a piñata? It's a colorful, candy-filled container that you smash open with a stick while blindfolded. Best. Party. Ever.

- ★ **Denmark:** If you're unmarried on your 25th birthday, your friends might cover you in cinnamon as a "fun" tradition. (Bring a towel.)

- ★ **South Korea:** Birthdays aren't complete without seaweed soup! It's a special dish meant to bring health and happiness.

Fun Fact: In the Netherlands, they celebrate "crown birthdays," which are extra special milestones when you turn ages like 5, 10, 15, or 20.

Saying "I Love You" Around the World

Love is universal, but saying "I love you" can look (and sound) very different depending on the culture.

★ **France:** Couples often say "Je t'aime" (zheh-tem) and share romantic gestures like writing love notes.

★ **Japan:** People might not say "I love you" out loud but show love through actions, like giving thoughtful gifts.

★ **New Zealand:** The Māori express love with a *hongi* (nose press) or by carving intricate wooden gifts called *taonga*.

Fun Fact: In the Philippines, there's a romantic tradition called *harana,* where someone serenades the person they love with a song. Swoon!

Family Traditions

Every culture has unique ways of spending time with family, from holiday traditions to everyday rituals.

★ **Italy:** Sunday dinners are a BIG deal, with families gathering for feasts that last for hours. Pass the pasta!

★ **China:** During Lunar New Year, families gather to make dumplings together. The more dumplings you make, the luckier your year will be.

★ **Finland:** Families love relaxing in saunas together—it's like a warm, steamy family meeting.

Fun Fact: In Ghana, families often name their babies based on the day of the week they were born. If you're born on Monday, your name might be "Kwadwo" or "Adwoa."

Music and Dance

Music and dance are a huge part of culture, and every country has its own unique styles.

★ **Brazil:** The samba is a lively, colorful dance that's a big part of Carnival, Brazil's biggest celebration.

★ **Ireland:** Irish step dancing involves quick, intricate footwork and dancers with the most impressive legs you've ever seen.

★ **West Africa:** Drumming is a key part of celebrations, and each drumbeat tells a story or shares a message.

Fun Fact: In Spain, flamenco dancers use their hands, feet, and even clapping to tell dramatic stories through movement.

Tea Traditions: More Than Just a Drink

Tea isn't just a beverage—it's a cultural experience in many parts of the world.

- ★ **Japan:** A tea ceremony, called *chanoyu,* is a peaceful, meditative ritual where every movement is carefully planned.

- ★ **England:** Afternoon tea is a fancy tradition with tiny sandwiches, scones, and plenty of tea (with milk, of course).

- ★ **Morocco:** Mint tea is served in tall glasses, and it's poured from a high distance to create bubbles on top.

Fun Fact: In China, tea is often served as a way to show respect, especially during important family gatherings.

The world knows how to party, and some festivals are so incredible they'll make you want to pack your bags and join in.

- ★ **Thailand:** The Yi Peng Lantern Festival fills the sky with thousands of glowing lanterns. It's like a dream come true.

- ★ **Scotland:** At Hogmanay, their New Year's celebration, people swing giant fireballs through the streets. (It's as epic as it sounds!)

- ★ **India:** During Navratri, people dance for nine nights to honor the goddess Durga. The colorful outfits and energetic moves are amazing.

Fun Fact: In Spain, during Carnival, people wear the wildest costumes you've ever seen—think feathers, sequins, and giant hats!

Unique Sports and Games

Sports aren't just about soccer or basketball. Around the world, people play some truly unique games.

- ★ **Finland:** There's a sport called *wife carrying,* where husbands carry their wives through an obstacle course. The prize? The wife's weight in beer!

- ★ **Japan:** *Sumo wrestling* is a centuries-old tradition where massive wrestlers try to push each other out of a ring.
- ★ **New Zealand:** Rugby is HUGE, and before games, the players perform a haka, a traditional Māori dance that's part battle cry, part team spirit.

Fun Fact: In Scotland, people compete in the Highland Games, which includes tossing giant logs called cabers.

Symbols of Luck

Every culture has symbols or items that are believed to bring good luck.

- ★ **Ireland:** The four-leaf clover is a famous lucky charm.
- ★ **China:** The number 8 is considered lucky because it sounds like the word for "wealth."
- ★ **Mexico:** Hanging chili peppers (called *ristras*) near your door is believed to bring good fortune and ward off bad vibes.

Fun Fact: In Japan, cats with raised paws, called *maneki-neko*, are thought to bring good luck.

Earth Wonders

Did you know that our planet is like a giant treasure chest, filled with wonders waiting to be discovered?

1. The Boiling River of the Amazon

Deep in the Amazon rainforest, there's a river so hot it can cook anything that falls into it. Seriously—it's like nature's soup pot!

What's Happening?

The river, called Shanay-Timpishka, is heated by geothermal energy from deep underground. Temperatures can reach up to 200°F, which is hot enough to scald your skin.

Fun Fact: Despite the heat, some animals, like birds and insects, still hang out near the river's steamy edges. Talk about tough!

2. Giant's Causeway: Nature's Puzzle

In Northern Ireland, there's a place that looks like it was built by a giant. It's called the Giant's Causeway, and it's made up of thousands of hexagonal basalt columns that fit together like a perfect puzzle.

What's Happening?

Millions of years ago, volcanic lava cooled and cracked into these amazing shapes.

Fun Fact: According to legend, the columns were built by a giant named Finn McCool to fight another giant in Scotland. Giants having beef? Classic.

3. Glowworms in New Zealand

Imagine walking into a dark cave and looking up to see… stars? Nope, those twinkling lights are glowworms! The Waitomo Caves in New Zealand are home to thousands of these glowing critters.

What's Happening?

Glowworms produce a bluish-green light to attract prey. It's like nature's version of a glow stick.

Fun Fact: The glowworms' lights are so bright that they can light up the entire cave, creating a magical, starry sky underground.

4. The Salar de Uyuni: Earth's Giant Mirror

In Bolivia, there's a salt flat called Salar de Uyuni that turns into the world's largest mirror when it rains. It's so reflective that it looks like the sky and ground have become one.

What's Happening?

The flat is covered in a layer of water that creates a perfect reflection. It's so flat and smooth that it's used to calibrate satellites!

Fun Fact: Salar de Uyuni is also home to giant cacti that grow on islands in the middle of the salt flat.

5. Stone Forest in China

In Yunnan Province, China, there's a "forest" made entirely of stone. The Stone Forest looks like a forest of rock trees sprouting from the ground.

What's Happening?

Millions of years of erosion carved these towering rock formations into their unique shapes.

Fun Fact: The local legend says the Stone Forest was created when a magical being turned an entire real forest into stone.

6. The Door to Hell

Yes, you read that right. In Turkmenistan, there's a fiery crater called the Door to Hell that's been burning for over 50 years. It looks like a portal to another world!

What's Happening?

The crater was accidentally created when scientists were drilling for natural gas in the 1970s. They lit the gas to burn it off, but the fire never went out.

Fun Fact: The crater is about 230 feet wide—big enough to fit a jumbo jet!

7. Chocolate Hills in the Philippines

In the Philippines, there's a group of over 1,000 hills that look like giant scoops of chocolate ice cream. They're called the Chocolate Hills, and they're a sweet sight to see!

What's Happening?

During the dry season, the grass covering the hills turns brown, making them look like chocolate.

Fun Fact: Local legends say the hills were created when giants had a food fight. (Who knew giants loved chocolate?)

8. The Underwater Waterfall in Mauritius

Off the coast of Mauritius, it looks like there's a waterfall plunging deep into the ocean. But here's the twist: it's an optical illusion!

What's Happening?

The "waterfall" effect is caused by sand and silt being pulled down the ocean floor by underwater currents.

Fun Fact: This mind-bending illusion can only be seen from above, so you'll need a drone or a plane to check it out.

9. Blood Falls in Antarctica

Remember the creepy red waterfall from the last chapter? Let's dive a little deeper. Blood Falls is one of Antarctica's spookiest wonders, and its bright red color makes it look like something out of a horror movie.

What's Happening?

The red color comes from iron-rich water that oxidizes (rusts) when it hits the air.

Fun Fact: Even though Antarctica is freezing, the water in Blood Falls is so salty that it doesn't freeze.

10. The Eternal Flame Waterfall

In Chestnut Ridge Park, New York, there's a waterfall with a flame burning right behind it. Water and fire together? How is this even possible?

What's Happening?

The flame is fueled by natural gas that seeps out of the rock behind the waterfall.

Fun Fact: If the flame goes out, hikers can relight it with a match. It's like nature's version of a pilot light!

If you think your school fence is big, wait until you hear about the Great Wall of China. This wall stretches over 13,000 miles—long enough to wrap around the Earth halfway! It's like the ultimate "stay out" sign.

What's Happening?

The wall was built to protect ancient China from invaders. It took hundreds of years and millions of workers to complete.

Fun Fact: Despite the myth, you can't actually see the Great Wall from space. But it's still one of the most impressive structures ever built!

2. The Pyramids of Giza: Egypt's Timeless Mystery

The pyramids of Giza are over 4,500 years old and still standing strong. These massive stone structures were built as tombs for pharaohs, and no one knows exactly how the ancient Egyptians built them without cranes or trucks.

What's Happening?

The largest pyramid, the Great Pyramid, is made of about 2.3 million stone blocks, each weighing as much as an elephant. Talk about heavy lifting!

Fun Fact: The Great Pyramid was the tallest man-made structure in the world for over 3,800 years.

3. The Eiffel Tower: Paris's Shining Star

Bonjour! The Eiffel Tower is one of the most famous landmarks in the world, and it's a shining symbol of Paris, France. Built in 1889, it was originally meant to be temporary—but people loved it so much, it stayed.

What's Happening?

The tower is made of iron and stands 1,083 feet tall. At night, it lights up with sparkling lights that make it look like it's covered in diamonds.

Fun Fact: The Eiffel Tower grows taller in summer because heat makes the metal expand!

4. The Colosseum: Ancient Rome's Arena

In Rome, Italy, there's a giant stone amphitheater called the Colosseum. It's like the original sports stadium, where ancient Romans gathered to watch gladiators fight (and maybe cheer for a lion or two).

What's Happening?

The Colosseum could hold up to 50,000 people and even had a retractable roof made of canvas. Fancy!

Fun Fact: Some gladiators became celebrities, just like today's sports stars.

5. Machu Picchu: The Hidden City

High up in the Andes Mountains of Peru, you'll find Machu Picchu, an ancient city built by the Inca people. It's so well hidden that it wasn't discovered by outsiders until 1911!

What's Happening?

The city is made of stone buildings, terraces, and pathways, all built without modern tools. The Inca were masters of engineering.

Fun Fact: The stones of Machu Picchu fit together so perfectly that you can't even slide a piece of paper between them.

6. The Panama Canal: Connecting Oceans

The Panama Canal is like the shortcut of all shortcuts. It's a man-made waterway in Central America that connects the Atlantic and Pacific Oceans, saving ships from a long, dangerous trip around South America.

What's Happening?

The canal uses a system of locks to raise and lower ships as they pass through. It's like an elevator for boats!

Fun Fact: Over 14,000 ships pass through the Panama Canal every year.

7. The Burj Khalifa: Touching the Sky

In Dubai, there's a building so tall it looks like it's trying to poke the clouds. The Burj Khalifa is the tallest building in the world, standing at an incredible 2,717 feet. That's like stacking 828 giraffes on top of each other!

What's Happening?

The Burj Khalifa has 163 floors and an elevator that travels at 22 mph. (Imagine zipping up to the top in seconds!)

Fun Fact: The tip of the Burj Khalifa can sway several feet in the wind. Don't worry—it's designed to do that.

8. The Golden Gate Bridge

The Golden Gate Bridge in San Francisco, California, is one of the most photographed bridges in the world. Its bright orange-red color stands out against the blue water and foggy skies.

What's Happening?

The bridge is nearly 2 miles long and connects San Francisco to Marin County. It's strong enough to withstand earthquakes and fierce winds.

Fun Fact: The Golden Gate Bridge isn't actually golden—its name comes from the Golden Gate Strait, the waterway it spans.

9. Stonehenge: A Mysterious Circle

In England, there's a circle of massive stone slabs called Stonehenge. No one knows exactly why it was built, but some think it was used as a calendar or a place for ceremonies.

What's Happening?

The stones are so big that people believe they were moved using sledges, ropes, and a whole lot of teamwork.

Fun Fact: Some of the stones came from 150 miles away, and scientists still don't know how they got there.

10. The Taj Mahal: A Monument to Love

The Taj Mahal in India is one of the most beautiful buildings in the world. It was built by Emperor Shah Jahan as a tribute to his beloved wife, Mumtaz Mahal.

What's Happening?

The Taj Mahal is made of white marble that sparkles in the sunlight. It's surrounded by gardens, fountains, and reflecting pools.

Fun Fact: The Taj Mahal changes color throughout the day, from pink in the morning to golden at sunset.

The Underground City of Derinkuyu

Location: Turkey **Secret Status:** A whole city UNDER the ground!

Imagine living in an underground city that's 18 stories deep! That's exactly what people did in Derinkuyu. This ancient city could fit 20,000 people and had everything they needed:

- ★ Schools
- ★ Food stores
- ★ Animal stables

★ Even underground churches!

Fun Fact: They had a giant stone door that could be closed from the inside to keep out enemies. Talk about the ultimate pillow fort!

Build Your Own Underground City Model: *Safe activity with adult help:*

1.   Get a big cardboard box

2.   Cut different levels into it

3.   Add tiny rooms and tunnels

4.   Use LED lights to light it up (Just don't try digging any real underground rooms!)

The Hidden Beach of Mexico

Location: Marieta Islands, Mexico **Secret Status:** A beach inside a hole!

Imagine a perfect beach hidden inside a giant hole, with a secret tunnel leading to it! That's Playa del Amor (Hidden Beach) for you. It's like Mother Nature and humans accidentally created the world's coolest swimming pool!

How It Was Made:

1.   Military used the area for target practice (not the best idea!)

2.   Their bombs created a huge hole

3.   Nature took over and made it beautiful

4.   Now it's a secret paradise!

China's Rainbow Mountains That Humans Built! 🌈

Location: Zhangye Danxia, China **Secret Status:** Not actually painted (but looks like it was!)

These mountains look like someone took giant paint brushes to them, but they're actually:

- ★ Made from different colored rocks
- ★ Pushed up by Earth's movements
- ★ Carved by wind and rain
- ★ Protected by humans to stay colorful!

The Crystal Cave of Giants 💎

Location: Chihuahua, Mexico **Secret Status:** A cave full of crystals taller than your house!

Deep underground, there's a cave filled with crystals so big you could:

- ★ Use them as slides (if they weren't so sharp!)
- ★ Build a house out of them (if you could move them!)
- ★ Play hide and seek behind them (if it wasn't so hot down there!)

Make Your Own Crystals: *Safe experiment with adult supervision:*

1. Mix Epsom salts with hot water
2. Pour into a clean jar
3. Let it cool overnight

4.   Watch crystals form! (They won't be house-sized, but still cool!)

The Secret Underwater Museum

Location: Cancún, Mexico **Secret Status:** Art gallery under the sea!

Imagine swimming through an art gallery! This underwater museum has:

- ★ Over 500 statues

- ★ Life-sized human figures

- ★ A whole car! Everything is covered in coral and sea life - it's like the ocean decided to redecorate!

The Great Wall's Secret Sister

Location: Kumbhalgarh, India **Secret Status:** The second-longest wall in the world!

Everyone knows about the Great Wall of China, but this wall is:

- ★ 36 kilometers long

- ★ Wide enough for eight horses to ride side by side

- ★ Has 360 temples inside it!

Underground Gardens of Fresno

Location: California, USA **Secret Status:** A paradise garden built underground!

One man spent 40 years digging underground to create:

- ★ Beautiful gardens

- ★ Fruit trees that grow underground

- ★ A cool place to escape the heat All because he didn't want to water his plants too much!

The Hand in the Desert ✋

Location: Chile **Secret Status:** A giant hand reaching out of the sand!

Imagine driving through the desert and suddenly seeing a giant hand sticking out of the ground! It's:

- ★ 36 feet tall

- ★ Made of cement and iron

- ★ Looks like a giant playing hide and seek got stuck!

Did You Know?

- ★ The Underground City of Derinkuyu was discovered when someone knocked down a wall in their basement!

- ★ The Hidden Beach was a military accident that turned into a tourist attraction

- ★ The Crystal Cave is so hot (136°F/58°C) that people can only visit for a few minutes!

Make Your Own Secret Wonder!

Design your own hidden place:

1. Draw your secret wonder

2. Decide what makes it special

3.   Think about how people would find it

4.   Share your design with friends!

Safety Explorer Corner!

Remember:

- ★ Never explore abandoned places without adults

- ★ Stay on marked paths when visiting wonder sites

- ★ Take pictures, leave only footprints!

Coming up next: We'll explore the world's most mysterious abandoned places – where nature is taking back what humans built!

Quick Quiz!

1.   How many people could live in Derinkuyu?

2.   What created the Hidden Beach?

3.   How tall is the Hand in the Desert? (Answers are hidden... just like these wonders!)

Hey there, mystery explorer! Ever wondered what happens when humans leave a place and nature moves in? Get ready to discover some of the most amazing abandoned places where trees grow through windows, vines climb up walls, and animals make luxury apartments out of old buildings!

The Lost City of Pripyat ❀

Location: Ukraine **Status:** A city where time stopped in 1986

Imagine an entire city where:

* ★ Ferris wheels never turn
* ★ Schools still have homework on the chalkboards
* ★ Trees grow through floors
* ★ Nature is slowly eating the buildings!

This city was abandoned because of the Chernobyl accident, and now it's like a time capsule where nature is the boss! Wildlife like wolves, deer, and even bears now roam the streets where cars once drove.

Fun Fact: The trees here are taking over so fast that scientists say the whole city might be a forest in another 50 years!

Make Your Own Nature Takes Over Scene!

Safe art activity:

1.   Draw a building (house, school, whatever you like!)

2.   Add plants growing all over it

3.   Draw animals moving in

4.   Give your abandoned place a cool name!

Hashima Island: The Ghost Island ⚓

Location: Japan **Status:** An entire island city left to the seagulls!

This island used to be packed with more people per square meter than Tokyo! Now it's:

★ Home to thousands of seabirds

★ Covered in wild plants

★ Looking like a battleship made of concrete

★ Being slowly hugged by vines

113

Fun Fact: The buildings are so close together that the island looks like a battleship from far away - that's why people call it "Battleship Island"!

The Underwater City of Shicheng 🌊
Location: China **Status:** An entire city under a lake!

Imagine an ancient city that's:

- ★ Completely underwater
- ★ Perfect for fish apartment hunting
- ★ Has dragons carved on the buildings
- ★ Looks like an underwater movie set!

This city was purposely flooded to make a reservoir, but instead of being destroyed, it's perfectly preserved under the water! Fish now swim through streets where people once walked.

Kolmanskop: The Sand Castle City 🏰
Location: Namibia **Status:** A city being eaten by the desert!

This old diamond mining town is slowly disappearing under the sand dunes:

- ★ Houses are filled with sand up to the ceiling
- ★ Doors open to rooms full of sand
- ★ The desert is playing the world's biggest game of "The Floor is Lava" (Except with sand instead of lava!)

Try This Sand Art: *Safe activity:*

1.   Get a clean jar

2.   Layer different colored sand

3.   Add tiny toy buildings

4.   Create your own miniature sand-taken city!

The Green Palace of Taiwan 🌳

Location: Taiwan **Status:** An apartment building turned jungle!

This apartment complex is now:

- ★ Completely covered in green plants
- ★ Home to countless birds and insects
- ★ Looking like nature's version of a luxury hotel
- ★ The world's tallest vertical garden (by accident!)

Ross Island: Where Deer Run the Government ☐

Location: India **Status:** Former British headquarters now ruled by deer!

This island used to be called the "Paris of the East," but now:

- ★ Deer walk through old ballrooms
- ★ Trees grow through government buildings
- ★ Roots wrap around old pillars like giant hugs
- ★ Nature is having the best house party ever!

Did You Know?

- ★ Plants can break through concrete with their roots!

- ★ Some abandoned places have become wildlife sanctuaries

- ★ Nature can reclaim a city in as little as 20 years

The Secret Life of Abandoned Places

When humans leave, nature moves in this order:

1. Small plants grow through cracks
2. Bigger plants break walls and windows
3. Trees start growing inside
4. Animals move in
5. The building slowly becomes part of nature

Nature's Detective Game

Try spotting signs of nature taking over in safe places:

1. Look for plants growing through sidewalk cracks
2. Watch how vines climb up walls
3. Notice how trees can lift up concrete

Safety Alert! 🚨
Remember:

- ★ Never explore abandoned buildings in real life

- ★ Stay safe by looking at pictures instead

- ★ Let the animals and plants have their new homes

- ★ Some abandoned places can be dangerous

Who moves into abandoned buildings?

- ★ Birds make nests in old windows

- ★ Foxes live in abandoned gardens

- ★ Bats hang out in empty attics

- ★ Even tigers have been found living in old buildings!

Quick Quiz!

1. What city was abandoned in 1986?

2. Which abandoned place is filling up with sand?

3. What animals now live in Ross Island's old buildings? (Answers are hidden somewhere in nature... or maybe just in this book!)

A Big Thank You!

Thank you for exploring The Book of Intriguing Facts for Smart Kids: Science, Geography, and Earth Wonders! You've traveled through fascinating science, discovered jaw-dropping geography, and uncovered some of the coolest wonders on our planet. You're officially a Fact Explorer Extraordinaire! 🏆

If you had fun learning, laughing, and saying "Whoa, I didn't know that!"—then guess what? There's more where this came from! I've got other books packed with even more mind-blowing facts, fun stories, and adventures that will keep your brain buzzing with excitement.

So, if you're curious about even more cool stuff, like wacky animals, space mysteries, or bizarre inventions, check out my other books! Remember, the world is full of wonders—keep exploring and never stop asking questions!

Until next time,

P.S. If you enjoyed this book, tell your friends, parents, or even your pet goldfish about it! Sharing cool facts is always more fun. 🩶